EQUINE BUSINESS GUIDE

5th Edition 2005

Editor
Richard Bacon

Research Assistant
Rebecca Wilkinson

ROYAL LEAMINGTON SPA | RUGBY | MORETON MORRELL

Distributed by:
Equi-Study
Warwickshire College
Moreton Morrell Centre
Warwick
CV35 9BL
Tel. 01926 651085

Published by:-
Warwickshire College
Moreton Morrell Centre
Warwick
CV35 9BL
(01926) 651085
www.equistudy.ac.uk

First published 1995 in conjunction with Welsh Institute of Rural Studies

ISBN 0-9510955-9-5

INTRODUCTION

The purpose of a business is to make money (although the proprietor may also have other objectives). In order to achieve this goal it is vital that the decision-maker has accurate and reliable information, allied to business acumen.

Warwickshire College has been involved in researching equine business data since 1985, when the first edition of the Horse Business Management Reference Handbook was published. This became established as the authoritative source for equine business benchmarking data. In 1995 this was brought up to date with the publication of the 1st edition of the Equine Business Guide, produced in conjunction with the Welsh Institute of Rural Studies. In this edition we have stayed close to our original intentions and have made revisions in the light of further research, to update the unique benchmarking data. A major change with this new edition is that much of the general reference material has been omitted: with widened access to the Internet this material is now accessible in other forms.

Pressures on equine businesses in recent years – litigation, insurance, competition, regulation, employment, etc. – all highlight the importance of managers being more than just good horse people; business skills have never been more vital.

The Equine Business Guide is a unique and invaluable management tool. However, its research and production would not be possible without the co-operation of the industry. As ever, we are especially indebted to those businesses that have offered data to our survey. *Without this co-operation, production of the guide would not be possible.* The "Strategy for the Equine Industry" being written by DEFRA and the British Horse Industry Confederation includes reference to the need for benchmarking data. We have now provided such data for a number of years, and will be happy to co-operate with efforts to increase the availability of reliable data to the industry in the future.

Note

In an ideal world, every piece of information would be correct, but Governments change systems, people change addresses, and we might have had an error slip through unnoticed. Please advise us of any corrections or suggestions. Also, although everything has been put forward in good faith, it is up to each individual to make suitable checks before committing themselves to risk on the basis of our information.

Suggested Reading

Horses and Money by Richard Bacon
Horse Business Management (3nd Edition) by Jeremy Houghton-Brown
    and Vincent Powell-Smith
Both published by Blackwell Science Ltd.

Health and Safety Compliance for the Horse Industry, published by Equi-
    Study Business School Series - contact the address on the title page for
    the full range of courses available.

Acknowledgements

We would like to thank everyone who has helped in the production of this edition, in particular the following organisations:

- Association of British Riding Schools
- British Equestrian Federation
- British Equestrian Trade Association
- British Horse Society
- National Trainers Federation

CONTENTS

Horse Business Survey Results

Introduction

This data has been collected from horse businesses of different types, spread over a wide geographical area. It is therefore believed to be representative of the industry as a whole. Among those surveyed were examples of very professionally and profitably run enterprises. At the opposite extreme, some were struggling to break even, and were often achieving performance levels well below those that may be possible. This fact is reflected in the results presented.

Where there is enough data, the analysis is extended from a survey average to include premium level of performance of the most profitable businesses within a business type. In previous editions we have included a regional analysis. This has not been included in the 5th edition, as the only significant trend has been that both prices and costs tend to be higher in the Home Counties and South East. Otherwise, there has been as much variation within as between regions.

Data Presentation

Gross margins

The results are presented in the *gross margin* format. This recognises that a business is often made up of more than one activity or enterprise. For example, a yard may own school horses and take liveries.

Each enterprise generates its own items of income. It also incurs its own readily identifiable costs, which depend to a large extent on the scale of the enterprise, i.e. the number of horses of a particular type kept. These costs are termed variable costs, and include items such as feed, bedding and veterinary expenses. The gross margin generated by an enterprise is its sales less the variable costs:

Gross Margin = Sales - Variable Costs

Gross margins must also make an allowance for any change in the valuation of livestock used in that enterprise, since ultimately horses will need to be replaced.

It should be emphasised that gross margin is not the same as profit. It does however provide a useful indicator of business performance for comparative purposes.

Net profit

As well as the variable costs, which have been included in the gross margin calculation, the business will also have overhead expenses such as labour, rates, fuel, etc. The net profit for the business is the total of all the gross margins plus any other income, less the overheads.

Net Profit = Total of gross margins + Other income - Overheads

Cost categories

Variable costs

These are the direct costs of keeping horses, which tend to relate closely to the number of horses kept. The headings generally used are:

Concentrate feeds	purchased hard feeds
Hay*	purchased hay, haylage and other forage products
Bedding*	purchased straw, shavings and other bedding materials
Veterinary and medicines	including wormers
Farrier	
Other	includes the costs of tack maintenance, entry fees, haulage, etc.
Horse replacement	this is the cost of replacements less the value of horses sold

* These costs are low on some holdings due to the use of home produced materials which are often difficult to quantify or value.

Overhead expenses

These are the general costs incurred in running a business, which cannot easily be attributed to a particular enterprise. Notes on the categories used are below:

Rates	business rates
Property repairs and maintenance	including buildings, arenas and fencing; buildings depreciation
Labour	including wages and salaries, staff training and National Insurance Contributions
Vehicles and equipment	vehicle running costs, repairs and insurance; fuel, oils; machinery depreciation
Office and sundry	includes marketing, fees, telephone and stationery, etc.
Insurance	General business insurance (not vehicles), including public liability
Rent	rents paid
Interest charges	interest and other finance costs

Survey Gross Margin Results

These are shown for a range of horse enterprises. In all gross margins, the figures relate to *one horse* of the type stated, over a *one year* period. Appropriate performance measures and prices are given where the data is sufficient to allow this.

Survey Whole Business Data

A consistent format is followed, with information under three headings:

1. Holding details

These are the average details of the data sample in terms of land area and numbers of different types of horses.

2. Profitability

This data is shown as:

	Sales	
minus	Variable costs	_____
equals	*Gross margin*	£
minus	Overhead expenses	_____
equals	*Net profit*	£_____

As with the gross margin results, all figures are *per horse* for *one year*, with the business totals divided by the *total number of horses* on the holding. The only exception to this is for studs - see the separate notes for this enterprise.

3. *Efficiency measures*

These are calculated to help analyse the performance of a business in more detail. Four measures are given:

(a) Gross margin %   = $\dfrac{\text{Gross margin} \times 100}{\text{Sales}}$

A low figure indicates that sale prices are low and/or variable costs are too high for the performance achieved. For example, consider the following figures:

	Your holding £/horse/year	Survey average £/horse/year
Sales	2,500	3,500
Variable costs	700	800
Gross Margin	£1,800	£2,700
Gross margin %	72%	77%

The lower gross margin percentage indicates that income needs to be improved, i.e. the relationship between sales per unit and variable costs is better in the 'survey average' than in the individual holding.

(b) Net profit %   = $\dfrac{\text{Net profit} \times 100}{\text{Sales}}$

If this figure is low, but the gross margin percentage compares favourably with the survey data, overhead expenses must be high. A figure of less than 10% should always be viewed with disappointment.

(c) Labour efficiency (Sales per £100 labour costs)
$$\frac{\text{Sales} \times 100}{\text{Labour costs}}$$
This shows the productivity of labour in generating sales revenue.

Using the Data

1. For comparing the performance of a holding with that of the survey, to identify where costs and sales are different to others in the industry. Divide the totals from the accounts by the number of horses on the holding.

When comparing data, a number of points should be borne in mind:

- all businesses operate in different circumstances and have unique costs and income structures
- profit is only one measure of performance of a business
- check that the make-up of the business is similar in terms of horse numbers and contribution to total sales
- note that a small yard is likely to have higher overhead expenses per horse than a large one

2. The data can also be used as a guide for likely costs and returns when budgeting an enterprise.

Livery

Livery provision is often subsidiary or complementary to other business activities, commonly a riding school, competition yard or farm.

In keeping with many other equine pursuits, recent years have seen a growth in demand for livery provision. This has been partly met by equestrian establishments and also by farm diversification into stabling. The advantageous status of farms regarding rates is a concern to many established businesses. The increasing availability of livery yards has resulted in a position where many operators have to improve standards to maintain their client base. Despite extra competition, livery charges have increased to counter rising costs for labour and insurance.

Livery services are provided under a number of different descriptions. For the purposes of the analysis, the following definitions have been applied:

Full livery

Full care of the horse, including exercise. More specialist services, such as care of hunters and breaking, are also included.

Part livery

Full care, excluding exercise.

DIY livery

The provision of stable only, with daily care and exercise attended to by the owner.

Grass livery

Horses kept at grass, often only on a seasonal basis

Livery fees	Average £/week	Range
Breaking / hunter	130	90-155
Full livery	86	50-120
Part livery	65	30-90
DIY livery	26	18-50
Grass livery	18	10-30

A very wide range in charges is found. More innovative yards base the charge specifically to the requirements of a particular horse rather than having a standard list price.

Performance targets - livery enterprises

	Full livery	Part livery	DIY livery	Grass livery
Fee (£/week)	£100	£75	£30	£24
Uptake (weeks/year)	45	45	45	26
Sales		*£ / livery / year*		
Livery fees	4,500	3,375	1,350	624
Other	100	100	100	50
	4,600	3,475	1,450	674
Variable costs				
Concentrate feeds	280	280		
Hay	250	250		
Bedding[1]	120	120		
Grazing expenses	15	15	15	30
Other	25	25	25	25
	690	690	40	55
Gross margin	**3,910**	**2,785**	**1,410**	**619**

[1] Straw bedding; shavings costs approximately £8 per week more, which should be reflected in the livery fee

Whole business data

The figures are an average for all livery horses, of whatever type. It is reasonable to expect a yard with mainly full livery horses to have a higher level of sales and costs per horse. Many DIY and grass livery stables are based on farms and manage to operate on a very low cost basis. The analysis illustrates the differences in cost structure between specialist and farm-based yards.

	Average	Top 25%
	£ / livery / year	
Sales		
Livery fees	1,685	2,334
Other	265	523
	1,950	2,857
Variable costs		
Concentrate feed	109	162
Hay / forage	150	111
Bedding	116	135
Veterinary & medicines	20	24
Farrier	24	34
Other	15	0
	434	465
Gross margin	**1,516**	**2,392**
Overheads		
Labour	377	339
Property rent paid	89	167
Business rates	47	41
Grassland rent / maint.	43	57
Water, electric & power	33	36
Other property expenses	96	79
Vehicle & equipment expenses	99	146
Insurance	29	28
Office & administration	84	99
Bank charges & interest	37	48
	933	1,039
Net profit	**583**	**1,353**

	Average	Top 25%
Holding details		
Area (ha per horse)	0.76	1.03
Horse numbers		
Full liveries	5.5	1.0
Part liveries	12.1	18.7
DIY liveries	16.3	24.2
Grass liveries	11.0	4.0
Other horses	2.8	4.8
	47.8	52.6
Efficiency measures		
Gross margin %	87%	90%
Net profit %	31%	44%

Race Training

The figures are taken from a mixture of Flat and National Hunt yards. Due to a low response to the survey, the 2005 figures should be treated with caution. Results from the 2002 survey are included for comparison.

	2005	**2002**	
		Average	Top 25%
		£/horse /year	
Sales			
Training fees	10,756	7,226	8,081
Other	2,505	531	850
	13,262	7,756	8,931
Variable costs			
Concentrate feed	704	493	435
Hay / forage	320	310	449
Bedding	577	466	505
Veterinary & medicines	1,200	301	272
Farrier	464	313	299
Other	551	92	56
	3,815	1,975	2,015
Gross margin	**9,447**	**5,781**	**6,915**
Overhead expenses			
Labour	5,713	2,788	2,565
Property rent paid	278	333	652
Business rates	189	111	84
Grassland rent / maintenance	19	36	7
Water, electricity & power	90	79	14
Other property expenses	308	154	66
Vehicle & equipment expenses	657	587	259
Insurance	137	76	60
Office & administration	386	180	215
Bank charges & interest	91	116	219
	7,867	4,459	4,142
Net profit	**1,580**	**1,322**	**2,774**

	2005	2002	
		Survey average	Top 25%
Holding details			
Area (ha)		31.0	10.0
Horses in training	61.0	22.1	20.2
Efficiency measures			
Gross margin %	71%	73%	78%
Net profit %	12%	13%	30%
Sales / £100 labour	£232	£286	£357
Racing performance			
Winners	0.75	0.53	0.56
Placed	1.49	1.97	1.99
Prize money	£6,466	£3,452	£3,273
Training fee £/week	£260	£182	£194

The racing industry has seen some positive developments in recent years, with expansions to the fixture list, widening participation in racehorse ownership, and improvements in prize money. However, concerns are still widespread regarding the relatively low level of prize money in the UK, staffing difficulties on yards, and rising business costs that are constraining profits.

Riding Schools

Despite reports in the media suggesting that the sector is struggling, our research since 2000 does not support this. A significant number of centres were struggling to be viable in the 1990's, and some of these have subsequently closed. In recent years the number of riding schools has stabilised, and most have experienced a period of expanding clientele and profitability. The main challenges have shifted from survival to the increasingly professional management needed by proprietors. This is required to cope with the increasing complexity of employment, regulation and the threat of litigation.

Since our last research, prices charged by centres have increased, but these have been necessary to counter significant rises in labour and insurance costs. Recruiting and retaining staff with suitable skills and dedication is a common problem.

School Horse Gross Margin

This is for all animals used in the school, including owned school horses or ponies and working liveries.

Lesson prices (£ per hour)

The prices given are for an adult rider on a horse. Childrens' lessons are often £1-2 per hour cheaper. Private lesson charges are influenced by the experience, reputation or qualifications of the instructor.

	Range	Average
Group lesson	10 - 35	17
Private lesson	17 - 58	29
Semi private	15 - 32	22
Hack	12 - 25	19

Working livery	Range	Average
Fee £ per week	15 - 69	42

The fee for working livery is variable, and often depends on the amount of use made of the horse in the school.

School horse / pony gross margin

Figures are expressed as an average for all school horses, ponies and working liveries (£ per school horse) over *one year*.

	Average	Top 25%
	£ / horse / year	
Sales		
Lessons	4894	6027
Working livery fees	241	302
Other	<u>940</u>	<u>2282</u>
	<u>6075</u>	<u>8611</u>
Variable costs		
Concentrate feed	112	194
Hay / forage	206	287
Bedding	106	168
Veterinary & medicines	229	299
Farrier	314	488
Horse / pony replacement	106	113
Tack, rosettes, etc.	<u>64</u>	<u>40</u>
	1138	1589
Gross margin	4937	7022
Lessons per week	5.0	6.3
Gross margin %	81%	82%
Lesson prices (per hour)		
Group lesson	16.78	19.10
Private lesson	29.03	35.50
Semi private	21.90	32.00
Hack	18.90	23.00
Working livery (per week)	41.91	50.00

Riding School - Whole Business Data (*per year*)

	Average	Top 25%
	£ / horse	
Sales		
Lessons, courses, hacks	2,754	3,307
Livery fees	851	1051
Other	<u>580</u>	<u>219</u>
	4,185	4,577
Variable costs		
Concentrate feed	111	132
Hay / forage	201	172
Bedding	103	125
Veterinary & medicines	129	84
Farrier	177	145
Horse / pony replacement	60	159
Other	<u>92</u>	<u>17</u>
	872	835
Gross margin	**3,313**	**3,742**
Overhead expenses		
Labour	1,366	855
Property rent paid	43	24
Business rates	81	92
Grassland rent / maint.	43	58
Water, electricity & power	71	90
Other property expenses	283	364
Vehicle & equipment exp.	193	262
Insurance	123	112
Office & administration	243	212
Bank charges & interest	<u>77</u>	<u>86</u>
	2,524	2,156
Net profit	**<u>788</u>**	**<u>1,586</u>**

Riding School - Whole Business Data (cont)

	Average	Top 25%
Holding details		
Area (ha)	16.3	55.4
Ha per horse	0.4	1.1
Business horse numbers		
School horses	9.6	11.3
School ponies	10.6	10.0
Working liveries	7.8	9.0
Other liveries	24.8	19.3
Other horses / ponies	<u>2.7</u>	<u>0.5</u>
	55.4	50.1
Efficiency measures		
Gross margin %	79%	82%
Net profit %	19%	35%
Sales / £100 labour	£306	£535

Performance Targets

The survey data for teaching enterprises demonstrate that many businesses operate at a poor level of efficiency. The gross margin information presented as budget targets indicates the potential of an efficiently and commercially run enterprise.

Performance targets - school enterprises

	School horse	School pony	Working livery
Average charge /hour	£20	£16	£20
Teaching hours /week	12	10	10
Livery fee			£45
		Per year	
Sales	£/horse	£/pony	£/horse
Lessons	11,520	7,680	9,600
Livery fees	-	-	2,160
Other	200	200	150
	11,720	7,880	11,910
Variable costs			
Concentrate feeds	380	75	380
Hay	240	165	240
Bedding	140	50	140
Vet and med.	150	150	75
Farrier	280	150	150
Horse replacement	100	60	-
Other	50	50	50
	1,340	670	1,005
Gross margin	**10,380**	**7,210**	**10,905**

Assumes:
1. Ponies kept at grass for summer
2. Vet & med. and farrier for working livery 50% paid by School
Working livery arrangements are very variable, so these figures should be viewed as an example

Equine Tourism

There has continued to be a decline in the number of traditional trekking centres. However, in line with an increasing market for activity holidays, provision for riding holidays has expanded, often at established riding centres. Equestrian tourism can be interpreted to include a wide range of activities, from visiting a race meeting to taking one's horse away for a week. This is viewed by many as a potential growth area.

Guidance figures for tourist related riding activities are given.

Trekking

From trekking centres or riding centres.

	Range	Average
1 hour trek	£12 - 35	£18
2 hour trek	£20-47	£35
Half-day trek	£30-90	£44
Day	£35 - 100	£60

There is growing interest in trail rides lasting for several days. Organisation of these usually involves co-operation between centres. A network has been established by Bridlerides for independent horse and rider, with rides from 2 – 8 days. www.bridlerides.co.uk. Long distance rides such as the Pennine Bridleway also create new opportunities.

Riding holidays

A list of centres offering riding holidays can be found at www.bhs.org.uk. Accommodation ranges from simple self-catering chalets to top class hotels. Prices vary significantly between centres, and also peak and off-peak season. Typical charges:

	Range	Average
1 week full board	£355 - 700	£500
Week-end break	£150 - 300	£200

Bed & breakfast

Farmhouse style B&B rates range typically between £20 and £30 per night.

	per night	Low occupancy 120 nights	High occupancy 200 nights
		£ per person place	
Sales	£25.00	£3,000	£5,000
Direct expenses			
Food	1.80	216	360
Repairs & renewals	1.00	120	200
Electricity	0.50	50	100
Advertising & admin.	0.80	100	160
	4.10	486	820
Gross margin	**20.90**	**2,514**	**4,180**

Self catering accommodation

Figures for a unit to sleep 3-4 people.

	£ per week	Low occupancy 20 weeks	High occupancy 30 weeks
		£ / year	
Sales	360	7,200	10,800
Direct expenses			
Repairs & renewals	40	1,000	1,200
Electricity	15	300	500
Advertising & admin.	100	2,000	3,000
	155	3,300	4,700
Gross margin	**205**	**3,900**	**6,100**

Capital cost of accommodation has a major impact on viability. This depends on the type of facility, state of repair prior to renovation, and specification of the accommodation. Likely range £40,000 for chalet type building to £100,000 for conversion of traditional barn.

Studs

Many studs are based on agricultural holdings, and so are able to produce their own hay and bedding at low cost. This is reflected in the enterprise data. There can also be savings in overhead expenses for these farm based studs.

Recent years have not been easy for horse breeders, with difficulty in achieving realistic sale prices for youngstock, and an abundance of stallions. Only the best quality stock have produced satisfactory returns.

Most of the studs in the survey are breeders of either Welsh / native pony types, or thoroughbred and sports / competition horses. The data is thus analysed on this basis.

Whole Business Data

Figures are expressed as the business total, divided by the number of stallions and owned mares.

There is a wide range in outputs and costs of different studs, depending on a range of factors including:

- Type of horse or pony being produced
- Scale of the enterprise
- The extent to which overheads are shared with or covered by other enterprises of business operations

Particular care should be taken when applying this data to specific situations.

Stud - Whole Business Data (*per year*)

	Average	Welsh / ponies	TB / sport
	£/owned stallions + mares / year		
Sales			
Stud fees	437	79	855
Livery	482	19	1,023
Horses / ponies	1,646	663	2,794
Other	212	64	335
	2,777	825	5,006
Variable costs			
Concentrate feed	249	96	402
Hay / forage	107	91	122
Bedding	44	29	59
Stud fees	639	0	1,279
Veterinary & medicines	299	78	520
Farrier	78	50	106
Horse / pony replacement	16	31	0
Reg fees	23	11	34
Other	86	111	65
	1,541	498	2,587
Gross margin	1,237	326	2,419
Overhead expenses			
Labour	869	28	1571
Property rent paid	149	0	273
Business rates	0	0	1
Grassland rent / maintenance	98	122	78
Water, electricity & power	41	19	60
Other property expenses	161	41	262
Vehicle & equipment expenses	207	197	214
Insurance	73	36	105
Office & administration	93	40	138
Bank charges & interest	71	12	120
	1,763	493	2,819
Net profit	**-526**	**-167**	**-400**

Stud - Whole Business Data (cont.)

	Average	Welsh / ponies	TB / sport
Efficiency measures			
Gross margin %	45%	40%	48%
Net profit %	-19%	-20%	-8%
Holding details			
Area (ha)	27.5	27.7	27.3
Horse numbers			
Stallions	1.7	1.9	1.5
Brood mares	7.8	9.0	6.5
Youngsters	11.2	14.1	7.8
Other horses	1.8	0.0	4.0
Own horses	0.9	1.0	0.8
	23.5	26.0	20.7
Charges / prices			
Stud fee	309	156	462
Mare livery / week	25	13	40
Sale of			
Foal / yearling *	6,363	780	15,667
2-year old	1,470	1,213	2,500
3-year old +	2,113	1,849	3,500

* This figure is skewed by high sales prices for Thoroughbred foals

Other Enterprises

Many yards generate additional income through supplementary enterprises. Some idea of the financial potential of these is given in the following notes.

Tack Sales

Usually restricted to sales of less than £10,000 a year. A mark-up of around 50% can be achieved - e.g. stock purchased for £100 is sold for £150 - although it is likely to be lower if turnover is small. Key issues are the careful selection of stock lines, and tight stock control, to avoid too much money being tied up.

Similar margins can be achieved from clothing sales.

Feed and Bedding Sales

Farm based livery yards are able to make a reasonable profit from the sale of home produced hay and straw. Resale of purchased feed and bedding is usually restricted to a mark-up of around 10%, dependant on quantity.

Tuck Shop

Confectionery can be sold for a mark-up of around 25%, and drinks for 50%. Larger yards may justify having vending machines. These are usually supplied by distributors, on condition that all stock is purchased from them. A commission of 15-20% on all sales is also taken by the distributor. For canned drinks, typical figures are:

	Pence
Sale price	60
Purchase price	30
Commission	12
Margin	18

Arena Hire

Indoor and outdoor arenas can be hired out to a number of people and organisations, not just for equine use. Wide variation is found in hire rates (£/hour):

Average	£18.00
Indoor arena	£15.00 - 35.00
Outdoor arena	£10.00 - 20.00

Transport

Yards situated near busy roads (such as motorways) may be able to offer a recovery service operating in conjunction with the local constabulary. The basic call-out charge is currently about £30.00, and there may be additional fees. Many yards also hire out trailers and horse boxes on a self-drive basis or will transport horses, charging per mile or for a set fee. Licensing and insurance implications exist where businesses undertake horse transportation.

Cross Country Course

Courses are usually available to hire and a per person rate is charged. Price is dependent on size and standard of the course, but usually starts from around £10.00 per round.

A number of courses are linked by UK Chasers and Riders (Tel: 01926 450049; www.ukchasers.com). The current charge for such courses is £10 - 15 per round with £15.00 annual membership.

Construction costs vary widely dependant on the standard or complexity of the obstacle, and use of available features and materials. Guidance costs:

Simple schooling fence	£100
Novice standard	£150-800
Water features	from £2,000

Novice - Pre-Novice course:

Materials	£5,000-10,000
Labour	£6,000-10,000

Equine Swimming Pool

Swimming pools and spa facilities are becoming more popular. The main users of swimming pools continue to be racehorse trainers, but competition riders are showing more interest. Location is important for success of these ventures, with a high level of use most likely in specialist racing areas. Jockey Club approval is important if the facility is to be used with racehorses.

Capital cost	£80,000, excluding cover.
Charge	£15-25 per swim (approx 10 minutes)
Likely use:	

       Average 25 / week
       High 50 / week
       Seasonal variation is to be expected

Rates	c. £1,500 in covered arena
Running costs	£5 / day

Shows And Competitions

The ability to run shows is determined by the size and type of yard. Much work is involved in organising these events, but profit can be high providing the prize money is minimal and the necessary equipment is already owned. A minimum of two arenas is required.

A wide range of activities can be arranged. Please note that appropriate levels of public liability cover are essential. The following provide illustration of possible income and expenses.

Dressage / Showjumping

Unaffiliated (per class)

		£
Entries	30 @ £7	210
Prize money	(£10,8,6,4)	28
Judges' expenses		35
Score sheets, rosettes		15
		78
Gross margin		**132**

Around 4 dressage classes can be held in a day.
Dressage in an evening will usually be limited to 2 smaller classes.
2 classes in an evening are feasible for showjumping.

Affiliated (per class)

	Dressage		Showjumping	
		£		£
Entries	25 @ £14	350	30 @ £8	240
Prize money	(£16,14,12,10)	52	(£15,12,10,8,7)	52
Judges' expenses		35		35
Score sheets, rosettes		15		12
Paramedic		-	Note [1]	28
Affiliation	£1.85 / entry	46	Note [2]	14
		148		141
Gross margin		**202**		**99**

[1] Paramedic advisable for SJ competitions, cost £110 / day
[2] BSJA affiliation £55 / day

BE Affiliated Horse Trials (one day) - Novice		
		£
Income		
Entries[1]	240 @ £58	13,920
Start fees	240 @ £10	2,400
Sponsorship		800
Trade stands		200
		17,320
Expenses		
Prize money[2]		2,124
Judges' expenses		250
Veterinary & medical cover		2,000
BE affiliation & entry levies[3]		1,600
Abandonment[4]		684
PA hire, commentators, XC control		3,000
Toilet & marquee hire		800
Catering		500
Course preparation, materials, etc.		3,000
Showjump coursebuilder & judge		250
Showjump hire		150
Printing & stationary		200
		10,258
Gross margin		**7,062**

[1] Up to 40 entries per section. Maximum charges (2005):
      Pre-novice   £52.88, £10 start fee
      Novice   £58.75, £15 start fee
[2] Per section of 40 starters:
      Scale 1 £450   Scale 2 £339
      PN (optional) lower £166, upper £323
[3] Affiliation £275 first day; £225 for further days; Entry levy £1 per starter
[4] Abandonment - 5% after deduction of levy on number of starters

Nutrition

Feed Prices

Feed Stuff	Quantity kgs	Average £	High £	Low £
High energy nuts	20	5.74	6.99	4.48
Low energy nuts	20	5.17	5.99	4.35
High energy mix	20	7.69	8.99	6.38
Low energy mix	20	6.40	6.99	5.80
Stud - Mix	20	6.53	7.38	5.68
- Nuts	20	6.01	6.58	5.44
Oats	25	5.31	5.95	4.00
Barley	25	5.56	5.25	4.20
Maize	25	5.78	6.35	4.40
Sugar beet pellets	25	4.70	5.25	2.98
Chaff	12.5	3.60	4.40	2.90
Alpha	20-25	6.79	7.90	5.34
Horsehage	Bale	4.85	5.95	5.00
Hay	Bale	2.75	4.50	1.50

Bedding

	Quantity	Average £	High £	Low £
Straw	Bale	1.80	2.50	1.20
Straw	Per tonne	80	95	50
Shavings	Bale	5.23	6.90	4.49
Hemp	Bale	6.75	7.75	5.95
Paper	Bale	4.40	5.00	3.60
Rubber matting	12' x 12'	400	380	225
	10' x 12'	340	325	195

Please note that bale sizes vary from brand to brand.

Horse Health

Veterinary Charges

	Average £	High £	Low £
Visit by prior arrangement	24.90	44.00	15.00
Emergency visit	35.50	49.50	22.00
Pre-purchase inspection	94.00	154.00	60.50
Combined tetanus & viral influenza vaccine	30.10	39.40	17.94
Equine viral influenza vaccine	24.96	35.25	14.12
Wormers			
Eqvalan	10.00	10.25	9.50
Furexel	9.00	9.80	6.69
Equest	12.50	12.87	12.45
Strongid P - sachet	4.15	4.10	4.20
Strongid P - syringe	8.00	8.52	6.90
Pyratape paste	7.69	8.00	7.25
Panacur paste	7.87	8.21	13.95
Panacur Guard	14.87	15.62	13.90

Worming of all horses should be carried out every 6 - 8 weeks. Frequency depends on time of year, number of horses on the pasture and the average age of horses on the pasture.

Teeth rasping	15.00	26.00	10.00

Teeth rasping can be carried out by a vet or an equine dentist.

Farriery

New full set	50.00	70.00	40.00
Trim	18.00	30.00	15.00
Remove shoes	24.00	40.00	15.00

Horses need re-shoeing or farriery attention approximately every 4 to 6 weeks varying with the amount and type of work that the horse does. The importance of correct shoeing cannot be stressed too highly. Providing a guide to the price of shoeing is difficult as it changes with factors such as how far the farrier has to travel, the number of horses being shod, and the type of shoe.

Equine Equipment and Tack

The following is a price guide to the type of equipment that is most frequently bought when a new horse is purchased. The prices have been obtained by surveying a large range of equipment both from tack shops and mail order catalogues. The highest and lowest prices have been noted and the average has been taken from all the figures obtained.

	Average £	High £	Low £
Saddles			
General Purpose	400	780	280
Showing	455	625	280
Dressage	750	1,200	300
Jumping	600	850	350
Bridle			
Snaffle	90	150	26
Double	164	300	28
Stirrup irons	45	90	17
Girths			
Synthetic	14	17	10
Leather	48	65	30
Reins			
Rubber	25	40	10
Leather	25	40	8
Leathers (adults)	43	60	25
Martingales			
Standing	37	28	25
Running	37	44	30
Breastgirth	45	65	25
Breastplate	60	120	35
Numnahs	35	60	10
Saddle Cloths	28	45	10
Poly pads	27	35	18
Bits - Loose Ring Snaffle	40	70	9
Boots (pair)			
Brushing	23	30	16
Overreach	18	30	5
Knee boots	40	70	15
Competition	40	50	30
Fetlock	20	30	10

	Average £	High £	Low £
Rugs			
Quilted	55	85	25
New Zealand	140	230	60
Cooler rugs	40	65	15
Day Rugs	55	80	30
Summer sheets	28	35	20
Surcingles - elastic/web	14	20	8
Head Collars			
Synthetic	10	15	5
Leather	45	70	20
Lead Ropes	5	6	3
Lunge Equipment			
Cavesson	42	70	15
Lunge Rein	11	15	7
Lunge Whip	11	15	7
Roller And Girth	28	40	15
Schooling Equipment			
Side Rein	21	33	9
Draw Reins	15	44	5
De Gouge	50	60	29
Chambon	45	44	19
Market Harboro'	60	69	20
Stable/travel Bandages (set of 4)	11	15	7
Travel Boots (inc. knees & hocks)	48	75	20
Exercise Bandages (set of 4)	12	15	10
Grooming Kit (Full Set)	40	70	11
Equine First Aid Kit	38	50	25

Buildings and Stable Equipment

Buildings

When building a new yard or converting existing buildings thought must be given to the types and requirements of buildings on the site. There are many buildings that are needed, some of which are specific to the type of yard.

- Loose boxes
- Tack room
- Utility box
- Isolation box
- General store

- Stalls
- Hay store
- Office
- Staff room
- Isolation box

- Feed room
- Bedding store
- Manure pit
- Garages/parking area

Stables design criteria

	Metres	Feet
Loose boxes		
Pony	3.7 x 3.0	12 x 10
Horse	3.7 x 3.7	12 x 12
Large horse over 17 hh	3.7 x 4.3	12 x 14
Foaling box	4.6 x 4.6	15 x 15
Isolation box	4.6 x 4.6	12 x 15

Doors should be a minimum of 1.2 m (4 ft) wide and 2.1 m (7 ft) high, with the bottom half of the door being no lower than 1.4 m (4 ft 6 in) for a horse. There should be adequate headroom with a minimum of 3 m (10 ft). In all boxes there should be a minimum of 42 m³ (1,500 ft³) volume per horse.

Stalls	1.8 x 2.7	6 x 9

Dividing partitions should be 2 m (6 ft 6 in) high at the front and 1.5 m (5 ft) high at the rear. Ideally there should be a minimum of 28 m³ (1,000 ft³) of air for each horse within the building

Gates		
Lorry gates	3 x 1.2	10 x 4
Hand gates	1.2 x 1.2	4 x 4

Size of storage areas

		Volume per tonne	
		m³	ft³
Barley straw	Small bales	11.5	411
	Big bales	18.0	643
Wheat straw	Small bales	13.0	464
	Big bales	20.0	714
Hay	Small bales	6.0	214
	Big bales	8.0	286

Small bale size 900 mm x 450 mm x 380 mm (36" x 18" x 15")
1 tonne of hay   ≈   44 bales
1 tonne of straw ≈   60 bales

Building Material Prices

Prices are subject to variation due to a number of factors.

	Specification	£
Steel portal frame building (per m² floor area) Frame, roof and foundations	*Span* 9m 13.2 m 18 m	95.00 – 120.00 80.00 - 90.00 75.00 - 80.00
Complete barn - 3m block walls & sheet cladding, concrete floor	18m span, 6m bays	140.00 – 150.00
Floors (per m²) Concrete (incl. excavation & hardcore) *Walls (per m²)* Concrete block walling	100mm thick 150mm thick 150mm thick 215mm thick	24.00 – 28.00 28.00 – 32.00 30.00 – 35.00 44.00 – 50.00
Timber spaced boarding	pressure treated	22.00 – 25.00
Roofs (per m2) Cement fibre sheeting Corrugate galvanised steel		19.00 – 22.00 11.00 – 14.00

	Specification	£
Roads (per m length, 3.2 m wide)		
Hardcore		33.00 – 36.00
Bitumen surface	2 layers	60.00 – 65.00
Fencing (per m)		
Timber, inc. materials & labour	3 rail	18.00 – 21.00
Timber excluding labour	3 rail	9.00 – 12.00
Permanent electric fencing		1.00 - 1.25
+ energiser		99 – 250
Pressure treated posts	1.5 m	1.00 - 3.50
Pressure treated rails		2.20 - 3.80
Creosote, per litre		1.00 – 2.00
Gates		
Galvanised	3.0m	150 – 200
Gate posts, per set		20 – 55
Wooden	3.0m	70 – 280
	3.5m	85 – 290
Gate posts, per set		25 – 35

Equine Buildings

These prices have been taken from manufacturers' literature. A high and low price is given for guidance as wide variations may be found..

		High £	Low £
Stabling - Prices <u>do not</u> include site preparation, base or drainage			
Loose boxes			
Single	3.6 x 3.6 m	2,400	990
Pair		4,545	1,800
Block of 3		6,660	2,540
3+ per unit		2,155	795
Corner Units	3.6 x 5.4 m	3,025	1,400
Tack rooms	3.6 x 1.8 m	1,035	525
	3.6 x 2.4 m	1,400	595
Hay stores/general purpose	3.6 x 3.6 m	1,695	900
buildings	3.6 x 7.2 m	2,995	1,400
Feed store	3.6 x 2.4 m	1,140	650
Field shelters	3.6 x 3.6 m	1,145	990
	3.6 x 6.0 m	1,595	1,330
	3.6 x 9.0 m	2,275	1,850
Schools			
Indoor schools (Varies greatly	20 x 40m		
with size/site/specification)		120,000	40,000
Outdoor schools	20 x 40m	30,000	10,000
Surfaces			
Wood	20m x 40m	600	300
Sand		200	400
PVC		950	600
Rubber		1950	1300
Horse walkers			
4 horse	10.8 m	8,000	4,500
6 horse	13.7 m	16,000	7,000

Stable Equipment

	Average £	High £	Low £
Feed mangers	11	15	6
Hay rack (corner)	22	30	15
(wall)	33	50	15
Weave grids	40	50	30
Door grids	45	60	30
Hay nets	4	10	2.5
Buckets (3 gallons)	3	4	2.50
(6 gallons)	13	15	10
Barrows	120	200	40
Shavings fork	16	25	7
Straw fork	18	20	15
Broom heads	10	15	5
Shovels (plastic)	15	19	12
(metal)	22	25	19
Feed bins (steel)	300	550	120
Fire extinguishers	75	95	60
Fire hose reel	220	375	170

Showjumps (BSJA specification)

Wings 6' (pair)	painted	137	60
	plastic	105	90
Poles 12'	painted	29	17
	plastic	32	24
Standing Fillers		110	85
Hanging Fillers 12'	2'6"	70	55
	3'		60
Gates 12'	2'6"	125	50
	3'3"	129	55
Water Tray		80	45
Cups (per pair incl. chain)		10	6
Dressage markers	set of 12	56	31
Showjump numbers	set of 12	100	45
Arena Grader		195	100

Wages

There is no formal wage structure that governs the entire equine industry. Wages paid to employees are, in the majority of cases, subject to negotiation. An employee will often receive benefits such as livery, accommodation and training etc. as part of their remuneration. Individual yards often have their own pay schemes or pay scales through which an employee can progress. The structure of these schemes is often determined by the level of qualification. Employers may also offer a bonus/profit sharing scheme relating to the number of hours or pupils taught.

In all sectors, employers have found increasing difficulty in employing capable and qualified staff. Even before the introduction of Minimum Wage there was upward pressure on wage rates.

The figures below are representative of the wages paid to staff of different qualification / experience. A wide variation exists between individual business and regions. Irrespective of the data below, it is up to each manager to ensure that the requirements of the minimum wage regulations are complied with.

Freelance and Casual Rates

	£/hour
BHSI	30 - 50
BHSII	20 - 35
BHSAI	15 - 25

Full Time Pay Levels

	£/hour	£/week	£/year
Level 4 (BHS 4, II)	8.90	356	18,518
Level 3 (NVQ3, BHS 3, AI)	6.60	264	13,718
Level 2 (NVQ2, BHS 2)	5.29	212	11,013
Level 1 (NVQ, BHS 1)	4.13	165	8,586

Labour Planning

Requirements and Planning

Labour costs per horse are usually higher than any other cost, so there is a need for thorough planning and control in this area. New equine establishments need to plan for a regular workforce. Established enterprises need regular checks on peak period labour workloads. Should the enterprise diversify into new services or facilities, it must have enough labour available to meet this increasing demand.

The amount of labour required by an establishment depends on a number of factors that must be considered before an attempt is made to calculate the staff required. These factors include:

- type of enterprise
- amount of horse preparation required
- number of horses
- peak periods
- breakdowns

- additional activities
- availability of free labour (e.g. family help)
- machinery and equipment availability
- illness

Exact labour requirements for a business are difficult to quantify, and will depend on its size and system in operation. The following tables are to assist the manager when planning the staffing of an establishment. Note that:

- the figures given are for one horse
- it does not necessarily take double the amount of time to care for two horses as it does for one, therefore economies of scale are applied to labour planning in these instances

Consideration must be given to the 'office' side of the business, especially as more establishments are employing staff to cover tasks such as taking bookings, ordering supplies and organising rotas. These tasks take a significant amount of time, and may slow down or interrupt staff's normal routines.

Standard Man Days

The amount of work needed to care for a horse can be expressed as a Standard Man Day (SMD) requirement (or, to be politically more correct, a standard person day). The workforce needed can be found by totalling the SMD requirement of the holding and dividing this by the working potential of staff. Consideration of seasonal variations and other points outlined above must be taken into account.

It is assumed that each worker provides 300 Standard Man Days per year. This is based on 6 days per week, less bank holidays and allowing for illness and holidays.

1 SMD	= 8 hours
1 worker	= 2,400 hours/year (300 days x 8 hours/day)
	= 25 SMD/month (300 days ÷ 12 months)
	= 200 hours/month (25 days/month x 8 hour day)

Guideline reductions to allow for more than one horse

Number of horses	Reduce standard by
1	0%
2 - 5	25%
6 - 10	30%
11 - 20	40%
21 +	50%

Examples: Calculations of staffing requirements (refer to Seasonal Demands for Labour table)

1.	3 hunters require 3 x 920 hours	2,760
	Less 25%	- 690
	Hours required per year	2,070

	Divide by 2400 =	0.9

Hence approximately 1 full time member of staff is needed, who is likely to have some spare time in the quieter months.

Seasonal Demand For Labour

(Hours per discipline per horse)

	Total	SMD	Jan	Feb	Mar	Apr	May	Jun	Jul	Aug	Sep	Oct	Nov	Dec
Full livery	660	83	55	55	55	55	55	55	55	55	55	55	55	55
Part livery	480	60	40	40	40	40	40	40	40	40	40	40	40	40
Grass livery	240	30	20	20	20	20	20	20	20	20	20	20	20	20
DIY livery	180	23	15	15	15	15	15	15	15	15	15	15	15	15
Breaking / training	900	113	75	75	75	75	75	75	75	75	75	75	75	75
Stallion	895	112	70	75	90	90	90	90	90	60	60	60	60	60
Brood mare	605	76	40	40	80	70	70	55	50	40	40	40	40	40
Foal 0-1 yo	280	35	30	30	25	15	15	15	15	15	30	30	30	30
Youngster 1-4 yo	480	60	40	40	40	40	40	40	40	40	40	40	40	40
School horse	1,200	150	100	100	100	100	100	100	100	100	100	100	100	100
School pony	960	120	80	80	80	80	80	80	80	80	80	80	80	80
Eventer	1,120	140	75	85	95	110	110	110	110	110	110	95	55	55
Showjumper	1,030	129	65	65	90	90	90	90	90	90	90	90	90	90
Dressage horse	960	120	80	80	80	80	80	80	80	80	80	80	80	80
Hunter	920	115	100	100	100	65	40	40	40	65	80	90	100	100

This data has been revised from that included in previous editions. Over recent years, centres have reduced the amount of staff employed to care for a given number of horses.

2.   8 riding school horses, with 10 hours teaching per horse per week

8 horses require 8 x 1,200 hours	9,600
Less 30%	- 2,880
Hours required per year	6,720

Divide by 2400 =   2.8

Hence 3 full time members of staff, or 2 plus part-time equivalent to 0.8, are needed.

3.

30 brood mares require 30 x 605 hours	18,150
Less 50%	- 9,075
Hours required per year	9,075

Divide by 2400 =   3.8

Hence approximately 4 members of staff are needed - some of this demand will be seasonal with extra help during the winter and at foaling

Labour profile

A refinement in labour planning can be achieved by calculating labour requirement on a monthly basis to identify seasonal peaks and troughs in labour requirement, as an aid to:

- planning core full-time and part-time staff requirements
- identifying additional seasonal needs
- scheduling staff holidays or training
- planning activities to utilize spare staff time at certain times of year

Each worker is assumed to contribute 200 hours / month, thus the grid lines on the example on the following page indicate one labour unit.

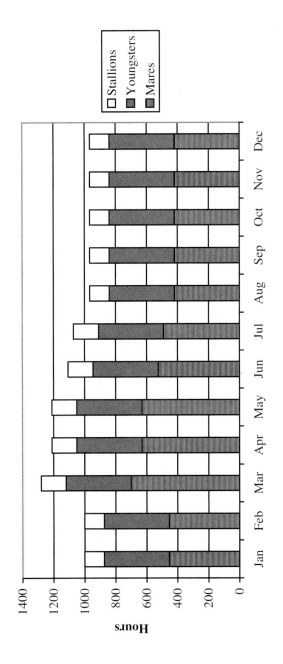

Labour Profile

Warwickshire College

The UK's leading equine college, with courses for everyone!

Full time further education courses:
Courses suitable for everyone – whatever your practical and academic background, including:

Higher education courses:
Foundation and Bachelors Degrees in Equine Business, Science and Horseracing

Part-time courses:
- BHS Stages
- Range of specialist subjects

Distance learning:

The flexible way to develop the skills and knowledge of yourself and your staff, with full tutor support.

- The Horse Care Series and Progressive Riding
- The Assistant Instructor Series
- The Intermediate Instructor Series
- Advanced Horse Knowledge Series
- The Business School Series
- Harper Adams University College Foundation Degree in Equine Studies

For further details please email equistudy@warkscol.ac.uk or telephone 01926 651085